To
Adèle Lots of love from Mum.
I will love you until
the sea's run dry
and time stands still.

**POETRY now**

## *FROM A DISTANCE*

Edited by

Heather Killingray

First published in Great Britain in 2001 by
*POETRY NOW*
Remus House,
Coltsfoot Drive,
Peterborough, PE2 9JX
Telephone (01733) 898101
Fax (01733) 313524

All Rights Reserved

*Copyright Contributors 2001*

HB ISBN 0 75432 684 5
SB ISBN 0 75432 685 3

# *FOREWORD*

Although we are a nation of poets we are accused of not reading poetry, or buying poetry books. After many years of listening to the incessant gripes of poetry publishers, I can only assume that the books they publish, in general, are books that most people do not want to read.

Poetry should not be obscure, introverted, and as cryptic as a crossword puzzle: it is the poet's duty to reach out and embrace the world.

The world owes the poet nothing and we should not be expected to dig and delve into a rambling discourse searching for some inner meaning.

The reason we write poetry (and almost all of us do) is because we want to communicate: an ideal; an idea; or a specific feeling. Poetry is as essential in communication, as a letter; a radio; a telephone, and the main criterion for selecting the poems in this anthology is very simple: they communicate.

## CONTENTS

| | | |
|---|---|---|
| Looking? | Jonathan Covington | 1 |
| Love | Dorothy Woodward | 2 |
| A Study In Red | Brian L Porter | 3 |
| Untitled | Anita-Marie Kilbourne | 4 |
| Collapse | Jill M Kimber | 5 |
| The Offence Of Defence | Lorand Tabith | 6 |
| Grand Design | Jeremy Jones | 7 |
| Purging Travails | C Thornton | 8 |
| Morag's Enormous Black Bag | Jean Tennent Mitchell | 9 |
| Untitled | Mike Fincham | 10 |
| Mulberry | Carole A Cleverdon | 11 |
| A Grain Of Sand | Robert D Shooter | 12 |
| I | Mary Mackinnon | 14 |
| An Insight To Motherhood | Gordy | 15 |
| Angel Love | Annie Overy | 16 |
| Friendship | Vera Walpole | 17 |
| A Memory Or A Day | Joanne Wheeler | 18 |
| Of This Kind V | Warren Brown | 19 |
| Missing With Intent | Margarette Phillips | 20 |
| Pale Face | Roseanna Tyrrell | 21 |
| Portugal | Wendy Poole | 22 |
| A Bed Of Rose Petals | Brian Wardle | 24 |
| Bluebells | Irene Hartley | 25 |
| House For Sale | Jane Solan-Robertson | 26 |
| Heaven Scent | Brian O'Brien | 27 |
| Eyes | Pam Dawkins | 28 |
| Perfection | Carole Hackett | 29 |
| Like A Flower | Nick Purchase | 30 |
| Grandchildren | Irene M Caine | 31 |
| Drought - A South African Poem . . . | Jane Finlayson | 32 |
| One More April | Frank Malin | 33 |
| Does Our Lord Listen | Will A Tilyard | 34 |

| | | |
|---|---|---|
| Books | Pam Eaves | 35 |
| What Memories | D J Price | 36 |
| Relief Road? | Debra Dawson | 37 |
| Days And Nights | Jason Davies | 38 |
| Johney | Dilys Mary Stuelb | 39 |
| Be My Love | Victoria Helen Turner | 40 |
| Outsider | Polly Davies | 41 |
| At My Father's Grave | William Ailbe O'Neill | 42 |
| First Love | Mary Ward | 43 |
| The Ploughman's Art | Les Merton | 44 |
| Horse Racing | Sylvia M Harbert | 45 |
| Come Be Seated At My Right Hand | Anne Hadley | 46 |
| Cruising Rock 'A' Billy Vampire | K M Clemo | 47 |
| The Woman With No Name | Dee Yates | 48 |
| Night Creatures | T Webster | 49 |
| My Lassie | L E Davies | 50 |
| In Kew Gardens | Terence Belford | 51 |
| Holiday Treasure | Vera Sykes | 52 |
| My Broken Heart | Pat Dring | 53 |
| The Great Race! | Roger Williams | 54 |
| Educating Susie | Pat Heppel | 55 |
| Room For Improvement | Mary Hodges | 56 |
| Alone | Tony W Rylatt | 57 |
| A Letter Home | Kayleigh Rhodes | 58 |
| My Home World | Margi Hughes | 60 |
| Not A Little Sparrow Falleth | Nicky Young | 62 |
| Maytime Magic | Dan Pugh | 64 |
| Dawn Raid | Joan Thompson | 65 |
| Family Photograph | Mary Guckian | 66 |
| It Was So Beautiful | Alma Montgomery Frank | 67 |
| More Than Words! | Lyn M Jones | 68 |
| Friend | E Osmand | 69 |
| Rush Hour Tragedy | Joyce Walker | 70 |

| | | |
|---|---|---|
| War Music | Robert James Berry | 71 |
| Your Baby Girl | Seph T October | 72 |
| The Dream | Sudha Patrick | 73 |
| Traces | John Tirebuck | 74 |
| The Runaway Horses | Kathy Buckley | 75 |
| The Aborigine And The Jewel | Margaret Bennett | 76 |
| Devonshire Downs | Joan Beedle | 77 |
| Spider In His Web | Kate Davies | 78 |
| The Clydesdales | Mary Lawson | 79 |
| White Silk | Mary Cane | 80 |
| Refugees | K Parveen-Mirza | 81 |
| The Renovation | Marcus Tyler | 82 |
| The Pain Of Fame | Ray Rippingale | 83 |
| Married Bliss | Edith Antrobus | 84 |
| Summer Time | K R French | 85 |
| The Soup - Tin Way | Peter Clarke | 86 |
| Football Plans | Catherine Craft | 87 |
| Trilogy Of Motherhood | Tina Coope | 88 |
| The Life Of An Unborn Child | Valerie Caine | 90 |
| Life's Progress | Jan Edmunds | 91 |
| The Face | D P R | 92 |
| Slender Harvest | Pauline Kirk | 93 |
| To My Two Boys | John Harrold | 94 |
| Who Would Have Them? | Jim Sargant | 95 |
| A Joyous Gift | Tess Walton | 96 |
| The Joy Of Children | Kelly Harding | 97 |
| Gold | Tracy Bell | 98 |
| Almost! | John L Wright | 99 |
| I Miss The Children | Frank Howarth-Hynes | 100 |
| The Joy Of Children | Jamie Brooks | 101 |
| Can I Wait? | Stacey Tully | 102 |
| The Parental Dilemma | Don Woods | 103 |
| To My Children | Ray Ryan | 104 |
| My Tiny Bundle - Oh What Joy! | Geraldine Varey | 105 |

| | | |
|---|---|---|
| My Grandad Keeps Penguins | Philip J Mee | 106 |
| Talking | Heather Breadnam | 107 |
| Precious Lullaby | Sarah Margaret Munro | 108 |
| Sali | Lloyd Hopkins | 109 |
| Summer | B Eyre | 110 |
| The Cottages | Sheila Maureen St Clair | 111 |
| The Tree | Vicki Turner | 112 |
| If Only | Jane Bolderston | 113 |
| Slaves Saved (Abridged) | M A Sanders | 114 |
| The Four Seasons | F Evelyn D Jones | 116 |
| Jack's Beach | Jean M Harvey | 117 |

## LOOKING?

We're all looking for an answer, answers that elude us?
One that is always hidden from us
but so obvious only a fool can see?
It's either fair or true
it's an answer that eludes even the wise?
For in tomorrow there is always a past!
Either for me or for you, if we look?
We must stand back to see
life's equation of the facts
of these hidden answers
which only a fool can see!
I find this entirely indifferent to me?
Seek and you may find?
Yesterday in tomorrow, tomorrow in yesterday?
For this life's riddle?
Is there a riddle hidden here or there?
Or is left up to you and me to decide?
Upon the things that are or will be!
Are we just bit part players in a game of chances
wishing for yet a better deal a better pay day?
That's left open for either you or I to decide
which road to take on our journey on life's highway
to where our destination is?

*Jonathan Covington*

## LOVE

Love is such a wonderful thing
It makes us happy and makes us sing.
A world without love would be nothing at all
For everyone needs it great or small.
Love is like a merry-go-round
It lifts you up and can put you down
We argue and cry like most people do
Then we love and make up with a love that is true.
Love is like the sun and the rain
It brings us happiness and brings us pain
It gives us the confidence everyone needs
To get through our lives with the greatest of heed
Love is something we all should do
Not just for ourselves but other folk too
It brings a warmth, a glow, a pleasure
And love is something we all should treasure
What would we do with no love in us born
No smiling faces to brighten the dawn
No happy laughter no music so sweet
All deep in sorrow, misery and defeat
That's why love is a wonderful thing
It does make us happy and does make us sing
All over the world love shines through
Giving a pleasure to me and to you.

***Dorothy Woodward***

## A STUDY IN RED
*(A journey through the mind of the Whitechapel murderer)*

Blood, beautiful, thick, rich, red, veinous blood.
Its colour fills my eyes, its scent assaults my nostrils,
Its taste hangs sweetly on my lips.
Last night once more the voices called to me,
And I did venture forth, their bidding, their unholy quest to undertake.
Through mean, gaslit, fog shrouded streets, I wandered in the night.
Selected, struck, with flashing blade.
And oh, how the blood did run.
Pouring out upon the street, soaking through the cobbled cracks,
Spurting, like a fountain of pure red,
Viscera leaking from ripped red gut.
My clothes assumed the smell of freshly butchered meat,
The squalid, dark, street shadows beckoned, and under leaning darkened eaves,
Like a wraith I disappeared once more into the cheerless night,
The bloodlust of the voices again fulfilled,
For a while . . .
They will call again, and I once more will prowl the streets upon the night,
The blood will flow like a river once again.
Beware all those who would stand against the call,
I shall not be stopped or taken, no, not I.
Sleep fair city, while you can, while the voices within are still,
I am resting, but my time shall come again.
I shall rise in a glorious bloodfest,
I shall taste again the fear,
As the blade slices sharply through yielding flesh.
When the voices raise the clarion call, and my time shall come again,
So I say again, good citizens, sleep,
For there will be a next time . . .

***Brian L Porter***

## UNTITLED

I'll never forget
The first time we met,
Nor the first time we parted.
And though there'll be pain
I'd do it again,
For I don't regret what we've started.

*Anita-Marie Kilbourne*

## COLLAPSE

It's very odd
  that I can nod,
    but cannot see.

    That I can blink,
      but do not think.

      That I can cry,
        but eyes are dry.

        That I can hear,
          but not my name.
          I wonder why?

*Jill M Kimber*

## THE OFFENCE OF DEFENCE

Defence or offence?
When do defence?
Turn into a serious offence?

The industry of defence
Cause a serious offence!
By selling offensive
Arms and armaments

Designed by experts
In the art of death
Sadly the victims
Are mostly women and children

To be politically correct
Profit is never considered an offence
The industry of defence
Cause a venomous offence
In the name of commercial
Business interest.

**Lorand Tabith**

## GRAND DESIGN

Shant'y band entice solo
opera act perform
to velvet curtain calls
thunders drum with violin
a wooden man'dolin.

Brass trum'pet metal wind
through French horns spar'kle
here tones and semitones assemble
to the scale that is ensemble
let music occupy our room.

A music stand for a note
across paper follow
looking for the crescen'do
a cello and bow
accom'pany one mez'zo sopra'no.

The conduct'or decree silence
now the gentle flute pipe
notes to hang in the air
that o'boe wood wind follow
that forge that is the mind.

Mozart compose upon the line
on a table quill ink and wine
the free gift of music
to occupy in joy
this or'chestra.

*Jeremy Jones*

## PURGING TRAVAILS

The pure joy of life, weeds out all the strife,
the pain or the anguish, gives way to the bliss,
of life never-ending, like eagle on wing,
majestic and soaring; look . . . here is the thing,
what Dante did teach us, no need for the rush,
to reach God's domain, like tide on the wain,
Hell you must go through, you'll realise its true,
kill all your despair, like hat that you wear,
turns black into white, to make what is right,
so, you will ascend, on that, can depend,
above the sun; beyond the stars, joy to behold: in joining the lars.

*C Thornton*

## MORAG'S ENORMOUS BLACK BAG

Morag! Morag! With your big black bag
this bag's her partner no matter how I nag
The simple reason its weight and so thick
knocks her off balance as she walks with a stick

All is in there but the kitchen sink
you don't believe me, well let me think
For a church meeting all she would need
a collection her glasses a card to read

No - she carries this enormous bag
after priorities, lighting a fag
Raking around a collection of purses
when you find her lighter somehow she nurses

Cigarette in her hand until it is lit
ashtray to follow, rake around for a bit
Cards for people, who have been sick
selected carefully as the words always fit

Lacquer make up, like a squirrel with a store
keys, paperwork and so much more
After the meeting once you have time
when you find her door key all is fine

Reminding Morag, leave the bag next week
to make it easier to find what you seek
She's so kind and gentle, makes you feel glad
but alas here's Morag with her big black bag

Filled up with cakes, biscuits for all
you'd be as well talking to the wall
Who could resist her, always their for another
I'll ignore the bag and just be mother . . .

*Jean Tennent Mitchell*

## UNTITLED

As we lie oblivious
The fridge hums
The clock hand turns
The fish swim around the lighted pool
Traffic passes outside by the dark street
The dog rests
The cat's eyes are closed

Meanwhile distant lights shine out
From the island of alleyways
The twenty-four hour supermarket
Is open for business
Inside, the food-laden shelves are vigilantly stacked
Outside, the store trolleys jig-saw together for continuous trade
Bread is constantly parked by the baker's bay

In the factory, the conveyor belt rolls on relentless
Lines of people chatter amid a metallic clamour
Uniformed staff patrol the aisles
Lights beat down
Noise radiates
Machinery moves
Hammers crash
Huge rollers grind on
Thunder fills the raucous air
Shouts echo throughout the length
And breadth of the building

But the cat still rests
The dog remains silent
And I am asleep.

*Mike Fincham*

## MULBERRY

Oh get off you silly cat
You try to love me
I try to read
You bite my book
I think, does it really matter

You have the loveliest of faces
With bright green eyes that sparkle
A coat so soft and black
I just have to sit and smile
At my little black cat

Yes, my little treasure
You win, my time again
I pamper you and cuddle
You purr and purr and purrrr
It's those big green eyes that do it
I fall in love again
With 'Mulberry'.

*Carole A Cleverdon*

## A Grain Of Sand

'In memory of Blair Gow'
the notice said in the shelter
'who died by accident when he was sixteen
while walking in the Welsh mountains he loved'.

I pause in my reading, turning,
looking out to the horizon,
my rush stilled seeking guidance
for the loss in the living sea
'this shelter was built
so that you too could enjoy
this place where he grew up
and knew so much happiness'.

I picture myself again at sixteen
on the foothills of life
my own four kids past that point.
'He has gone ahead a little while
and waits for us upon a stile'.
In other circumstances that language might repel
through it now though I picture him
he looks back and smiles at me
waiting for me, as if used to slower folk than he.

My moment in this shelter is an eternal one
'see you there Matie' I seem to say.

I grew up in other mountains
so I know what you found and never lost
happiness indescribable
which at least for one you have now passed on
enough to return and mourn your loss.

I smell fish cooking on the shore
bread being broken to hold it to eat
I rush to share and to eat
wiping tears away.

***Robert D Shooter***

# I

Oh to be free!
And set my spirit soaring
Rising on the wind
Of this fine September day.

Autumn it may be
But the sun is so mellowing
Chasing off my cares
On this fine September day.

Come fly with me!
From summer's endless toiling
Leaving children fledged
For this fine September day.

Now fancy free!
As springtime's love is waning
Demanding more and more
Of my own September day.

*Mary Mackinnon*

## AN INSIGHT TO MOTHERHOOD

Mother bird raising her young
loyal to her meaning
motherhood be the reason
this life have her done.

Raised into reality
that is, that you can fly
looking up at motherhood
as she guides you
to the sky.

Naturally unpoached
by those who think
know best,
left happy with
their family
left alone in their nest.

***Gordy***

## ANGEL LOVE

I hope again,
That I may heal;
The pain and heartache,
That you feel.

Thank you God,
Again I say;
Thank you once more,
As I pray.

Thank you for the peace
You bring.
No more the pain
Or suffering.

To mend your heart
And send you love,
Are little angels
From above.

Once more again,
I'll spend my day;
With you here,
Again to stay.

To write these words
Of hope to you;
And that dear Lord,
That we all may
Ever feel your love today.

*Annie Overy*

**FRIENDSHIP**

It really is a pleasure,
To send greetings warm and true
Remembering the years of friendship
We have shared with you.
Through glad days and sad days
Our friendship stood the test
Always there for one another
Hoping for the best.
Now it's time for celebrations
On this your special day
You deserve the very best
In every kind of way.

*Vera Walpole*

## A Memory Or A Day

When I was a child,
as I slipped my small feet into scuffed red shoes,
warm and familiar,
outside, bent over on the doorstep
under the blue-skied sunlight,
feeling airy and content.

Then, hearing what sounded like music, and
craning my small neck as high as it would go
straining to see the upper-most branch
of the largest tree,
with its chattering leaves
swaying under the morning sun.

And there, the smallest of birds sat,
singing with a sound so sharp and clear;
that it echoed the day itself.

*Joanne Wheeler*

## OF THIS KIND V

Mother of the quiet earth
Your love is so profound
Your light it carries all my worth
And in my heart it's found

You gave what cannot be taught
And forever I will explain
That your love I never sought
Though you bestowed every gain

You live with such a passion
In affection you truly believe
My life has been a lesson
On how love can be received

Mother of the proudest son
Your love never blinds my eyes
For your qualities are not undone
And your light brightens my skies.

*Warren Brown*

## MISSING WITH INTENT

No roses,
No more,
Not one for me to wear.

Is this as bad as it gets?
The poison of his and hers,
No money,
A missing car
An empty clothes peg,
Not a glimpse of an over-ironed shirt
Or a lap-top computer.

A multitude of untruths that hurt
The gossipers
Guessing the guilt
The explosion of lives
Concluding in stark divorce.
An empty space
In a cold bed
Thoughts jumbled in my head
My white wedding dress
Still hanging,
Nurtured with care
And me, free as air,
To cut it and tear it

No roses for me,
Not even one, to wear in my hair
And your chair
Still rocking to and fro . . .

*Margarette Phillips*

## PALE FACE

Like the pale faced insomniac
Who has got a fright
He looks out of the dark
Through a sea of
Tranquillity or crisis.
With his night-cap
Tossed sideways on
His waning head,
He shines and lights
Your night.

*Roseanna Tyrrell*

## Portugal

*I want to*
Swim in azure seas
Tread the golden sand
Taste salt on my tongue
Dive into the dappled pool
Jog on the jetty in the crystal morning
Lie on a sunbed daydreaming
Feel the morning fill my soul
Breathe heat and dust

*I want to*
Eat rock shapes
Jump in shoals of fish
Watch the red claim the land in the evening
Sit with friends in the cocktail bar
Siesta in the afternoon
Idle to cicadas
Savour food and wine

*I want to*
Choose peach juice
Wait for toast
Eat scrambled eggs for breakfast
Lunch on rolls and cheese
Look forward to chocolate with coffee
Bathe in pure white
Put my red dress on
Wake up the woman

*I want to*
Desire your lips
Kiss your heart
Reach your soul
Breathe as one all night
Wake in your arms
Watch you smile
Remember your words
Know love and pain.

***Wendy Poole***

## A Bed Of Rose Petals

Some moments cast gold plated memories
Some moments lay mother of pearl
But the memories in clear cut diamonds
Radiate round our sweet little girl
Her face like a bed of rose petals
Cradled in long golden curls
Sapphire eyes light the face of an angel
Her smile sweeps you out of this world
All memories now locked in an album
To live again in moments of leisure
Through the magic of a photograph album
You can return to lost moments
Of pleasure.

*Brian Wardle*

## BLUEBELLS

Bluebells there are crowds of them in the woods
Beautiful carpets of sweetly smelling flowers
Who plants them? No one knows
Do the fairies or the wood gnomes?
All we know is that every year in the spring
They appear in the woods and dells
Their broad green leaves and pretty blue bells.

Little children squeal with delight
When they come upon such a beautiful sight
They go down on their hands and knees
And pick bouquets so diligently
To take home to their parents so proud to give them such a gift
But the magical hand must surely be God's
He who makes everything so wonderful, so good
Even the flowers that bloom in the woods
Every leaf, every petal so perfect in detail
No human being could ever entail
Not just bluebells but everything there is
His tender touch, His gracious charm
That is the world we live in
But bluebells are best of all.

***Irene Hartley***

## HOUSE FOR SALE

Solid, strong and steadfast
But quiet and cold, I wait
My flowered walls call out to you
To walk in through my gate.

Dress my naked floorboards
And paint theses eyes of glam
That search in vain for masters' new
Among those who care to pan.

My mistress left me empty
After three score years and ten:
This heart of fire yearns to warm
These lonely rooms again.

Don't be harsh or nasty:
These walls and windows weeping
Will care for you when grief has gone
And guard your infants' sleeping.

Adorn my walls with portraits
Of your youthful family:
Tokens of your promise made
To breathe their life in me.

*Jane Solan-Robertson*

## HEAVEN SCENT

I love the smell of baking bread,
Fresh mown grass goes to my head,
The breathtaking bouquet of roses in bloom,
An open wood fire, expensive perfume.
The salty spray of a restless sea,
Christmas aromas, pot pourrys of glee,
But the greatest aroma is quite rare,
No other fragrance can compare,
The aroma you must work hard to possess,
The heady satisfying sweet smell of success.

*Brian O'Brien*

## EYES

Eyes for looking, eyes for peeping
watching, regarding, seeking
striving to scrutinise
- the sky.

Eyes fearsome, glowing, bright
as the tiger in the night
while other eyes are winsome,
tender
- shy.

From the calm eye of the storm
to its outer frenzied form
old Thor is such a
- tantalising guy.

Eyes that ogle, eyes that twinkle
and with that twinkle
wrinkle up,
perchance to hide
- a sigh.

How unnerving it would be
to waken in the night
and see, the green eye
of the little yellow god
- close by.

*Pam Dawkins*

## PERFECTION

The sound of happy laughter
Coming from children at play
The giggling and tittering of lovers
At the end of a perfect day

Kindness experienced from a stranger
The thoughtfulness of a friend
A favour returned by a neighbour
At the end of a perfect weekend

The delight gained from achievement
Satisfaction at reaching physical peak
A night out on the town
At the end of a perfect week

The greenery in the countryside
The colour of flowers in bloom
The sun shining in the sky
At the end of a perfect June

The celebration of a birthday
The wedding of a daughter so dear
The birth of a longed for baby
At the end of a perfect year

As a new year dawns
We can briefly reflect
On the time that has passed
And moments that were perfect.

*Carole Hackett*

## LIKE A FLOWER

The origin of life begins where the spark ignites,
ever illuminating and unfolding freely.
You can be subtle to the call
or evasive on the wall.

If ya feel it, say it,
if you don't, don't make it up.
Criss-cross. See the parallel.

My love sings a sweeter song,
flowing feelings come along;
I shake the hand who bites me,
tenderness in your caress unites me.
Past heroes. Present angels.
If I break away, think of love.

Stop thinking of it in dreams as a revelation,
but see it as true absorption; running, dancing,
past the waves and clouds into ever word-expressionless
bliss. So still and silent, like a flower enjoying
the child-like day.

*Nick Purchase*

## GRANDCHILDREN

Baby
blue eyes looking
at me wondering, thinking
walking away with disdain
and self-containment.

Long-legged
long-mane piercing eyes
lost in thoughts of horses
trotting, walking, cantering
galloping and jumping in the quiet
of home.

Strawberry red
blonde, wispy, ginger head
alabaster skin, china blue
eyes planning next attack on
dog, kitten, sister,
granny.

*Irene M Caine*

## DROUGHT - A SOUTH AFRICAN POEM
## CRY OF THE STRICKEN

Dry, dead earth, scorched brown grass,
Dried-up river beds, leafless trees,
Relentless heat, brazen and harsh,
No sign of cloud, no whisper of breeze -

The sun, like an inflamed wound in the sky,
Angrily tears the last flickers of life,

'Oh God our legs are weary, our lips are thirsty
Must our living still be strife?
Shall we never see again
The dreaming cattle by the dam?
Hear no more the gentle lowing
By the kraals at eventime?
Shall our little children never
Break the silence with their mirth?
Send us rain, we do implore Thee,
Drink to moisten thirsting Earth -
Our land is parched, its lips are cracked,
Will silk saliva never run,
To slake this torment on the rack,
This hideous pleasure of the sun?'

*Jane Finlayson*

## ONE MORE APRIL

Once more I prayed
From darker days, for the miracle
That makes winter worth the while.
And then before March passed

Front running young trees
Had flashed their wares, but faded
Like precocious two-year olds
Meeting the final furlong.

But older rivals battled on,
Saved for a time by sudden
Bursts of springtime sun,
Which did not last.

Somehow their colours were
A shade less bright than I remembered,
Like horses late with their summer coats.
But the fragile prints and greeny creams

Held on, with soft heads
Bent in defiant mourning
For their scattered brethren.
Then April came, sharp and cold,

And brought a perverse wind,
Which somehow missed its winter cue.
Death rattle in the branches,
Gossamer carpet in the gutter.

It had been a spring
Of fits and starts,
Aping my autumnal energy,
Fading when most desired.

*Frank Malin*

## Does Our Lord Listen

When we pray unto our Lord
Will He always hear,
We know He does, because we're told,
His presence is ever near.

He will not grant us all we ask,
Just give us what we need,
If everything we asked was given,
It soon could turn to greed.

Our Lord knows all our secret thoughts,
He cares for us night and day,
He wants us all to do our part,
And take the time to pray.

You do not have to pray out loud,
In places set apart,
He listens to you, wherever you are,
To your message from the heart.

Sometimes your heartfelt feelings,
Would be very hard to say,
But you need not be fearful,
He will help you on the way.

He also is our faithful guide,
As along life's path we tread,
So ask Him for your daily plan,
For He knows what lies ahead.

**Will A Tilyard**

## BOOKS

Just watch that child, see how he looks
Along and down the shelves of books.
He takes one out and peers inside,
Then laughs aloud, eyes open wide.

He turns around, his joy to share.
Then shoulders sag, there's no-one there.
Mum grabs the book from clutching grasp.
Her voice an angry, grating rasp.

'Oy, put that back, you can't 'ave that.
Can't waste good money on that tat.
'Ere, 'ave some crisps. I need some fags.'
Miserably forlorn, home he drags.

The tele blares. The adverts shout.
'Do your 'omework. D'you want a clout?'
His sad eyes peer through brimming tears.
Imagining the morrow's jeers.

*Pam Eaves*

## WHAT MEMORIES

What memories come flooding back - memories galore,
    When an old family album, one looks through,
So to be transported to the good old days once more,
    With some well loved faces coming into view!
One notices the fashions, how very much they change,
    There is Grandad's handlebar moustache - not small,
The stiff shirt collars, worn by men, to us now seem strange,
    Those bathing costumes, oddest sights of all.
Then we see top hats and stalkers, bowlers, trilbies, caps,
    Some ladies' Easter bonnets, feathered hats,
Plus fours, seen on Uncle Jack, the dandiest of chaps,
    To complete the outfit, round his ankles, spats.
But, whilst we note the changes, some things the same remain,
    Recurring family likenesses, we see.
Apparent through the pages, is one thing very plain,
    It is our very precious family tree.
That little family album, we never could replace,
    Yet the monetary value would be nil.
We thank the Lord Almighty for His everlasting grace,
    In the spirit, are our loved ones with us still.

*D J Price*

## RELIEF ROAD?

There's no end to the greenbelt destruction,
it goes on at phenomenal rate,
ripping up trees that swayed in the breeze,
which made our countryside great.

Nothing is as we remember, buildings and homes took away.
We're invited to speak,
though the prospects are bleak,
no one hears when we have our say.

In move the men to take over, to build our highway to hell.
Relentless they seem to shatter our dream,
as more trees they continue to fell.

Down goes the concrete and tarmac,
the road is nearing its end, no protesters in sight,
for they've lost the fight, maybe the answers around the next bend.
Relief Road?

*Debra Dawson*

### DAYS AND NIGHTS

Days go slow
Nights are long
I'll never know
Where I went wrong
I always thought
Your love was true
That you loved me
As I love you

So deep in torment
Where've I go
Nights so long
My days go slow
It was in you
I put my trust.
What you have done
Is so unjust.

Adultery, deceitful
Told so many lies
I've asked all the questions
Staring with why's
The answers
I will never know
Just nights are long
And days pass slow.

***Jason Davies***

## JOHNEY

We sat together our first day at school,
watching the teacher and trying to be cool,
    (me and Johney)
Climbed the mountains at eleven,
    (Johney and I)
No one had told me the wherefores and whys,
puberty struck, there were tears in my eyes,
    (Don't cry said Johney)
Teenagers now and off Johney went,
to fight for the cause of freedom and right,
    (brave Johney)
But we had our moment together, with the moon tangled
up in the trees, the stars shone down when we were one,
Johney and I and the night,
    (dear Johney)
He married soon after, a bolter they say,
made him sad and unhappy I'm sorry to say,
    (poor Johney)
Came home to retire, got old and then died,
I watched from a distance, kept away from the lot,
Didn't God say like the flower *forget-me-not?*
So I placed that blue blossom on his newly dug plot,
Wrote two little words that said the lot,
    (for Johney) x

***Dilys Mary Stuelb***

## BE MY LOVE
*(In memory of the glorious and great tenor Mario Lanza, 1921-1959)*

Your glorious melody,
Your song of songs,
From your heart,
Soared up to Heaven,
The sound of which caused joy and tears,
Bitter sorrow of love ungiven!
Song of your heart -
A cry from the soul -
Unbidden!
Be my love, you pleaded,
Our love was yours - forever!
Your spirit sang -
Until only your spirit sang on!
And our love has triumphed beyond
Your brief golden days,
And lives on with you in our hearts,
And in Heaven!

*Victoria Helen Turner*

## OUTSIDER
*(In memory of Becky. A true story)*

Am I welcome in your town tho' I'm from far away?
Should I try to fit in if I decide to stay?

I join this group and that, and try to be part
of a village whose name is now stamped on my heart.

'Are you planning to stay, Dear?' The question is asked.
'Yes' I reply, glad to say it at last.

As the days and weeks pass I begin to comprehend
a change in the folks I thought were my friends.

In the flock and clique all are friendly and nice,
but out on the street . . . they don't look at me twice.

I don't understand . . . what have I done wrong?
I thought I was welcome and tried to belong.

I'm dying of loneliness, I must get away.
Go back, where I'm from, I'll die if I stay.

I'll remember this town as long as I live.
The people I loved who had little to give.

Goodbye and farewell, I won't ever return,
to this beautiful village that has so much to learn.

*Polly Davies*

## AT MY FATHER'S GRAVE

The Mass was read, his deeds extolled;
Key moments of a life recalled.
Kind hands proffered and they were many;
The march of time cannot be stalled.
The church bell tolled our measured pace
As from the shrine the casket borne;
And each man knew as know he must,
One day 'tis him they'll mourn.
From where I stood close by my kin,
The graveside crowd fanned fifty deep;
Respects to the deceased for sure,
No less for us who weep.
Now, time had come for final prayers;
The priest held forth, delivery clear.
We joined his call for Christ's goodwill,
Intoned the saints our voice to hear.
Amid this solemn, pious scene,
My eye was drawn to grave-soil mound
Where Justin there was kicking clods;
Hurrah! Hurrah! - diversion found.
Or . . . maybe he was busting clay
For gentler fill where Grandpa lay.

*William Ailbe O'Neill*

## FIRST LOVE

My dearest one I loved you so much
I do so miss your gentle touch,
The way you looked, that secret smile
Will stay with me a long long while.

I remember the last time that we met
You hugged me and held me close
It was a day I never will forget
Because I loved you the most.

Then one day I heard that you had died
I just sat down and cried and cried
Death does not stop loving it never will
Because I know that you are with me still.

*Mary Ward*

## The Ploughman's Art

Like his father
he was a son of the soil
who loved to smell fresh earth

as he guided
the plough behind gentle giants
plodding forward on solid hooves

with inner strength
pulling the heavy plough
to slice and turn ground before him.

He was an artist
changing landscapes
from rolling green countryside

to furrowed lines
like an artistic mood
of the painter Vincent van Gogh;

who could also be
inspired by golden corn
growing from the ploughman's art.

**Les Merton**

## HORSE RACING

Do you watch the racing on the TV
I'm not one who bets, but I watch it you see.
The wonderful power of the horse's limbs.
Snorting out breath, as he tries to win.

With their ears erect, their eyes straight ahead.
Their muscular system working, a true thoroughbred.
Some have tails plaited and their hair from their heads
I prefer to see it loose, flowing in the breeze instead.

If he comes in first, I'm sure that he knows,
Although he sweats, his blanket they throw.
Over his back, so he won't get a chill,
He must not get cold, or he will be ill.

Horses must cost their owners a great deal,
Veterinary fees to the owner won't appeal.
To take great care of them, is their aim.
The horses are pampered from tail to his mane.

*Sylvia M Harbert*

## COME BE SEATED AT MY RIGHT HAND

The consent of the apple grower.
Why should he eat humble pie.
Why should he in fact eat anything at all.
He had always had to yield, surely he should
be left to do things his own way.
For a change he had made his own apple wine
and for a short time he had consumed it.
For a short time he had bathed in its glory
and now the novelty had worn off -
He had consumed and been found desolate.
Had considered and been found wanting -
His needs were so deep they were hidden in the
deepest well of despair.
He, however, did not want to come out of that
'well' and be wanting, so decided to stay in
that 'well' instead.
How can this situation be resolved you might ask?
How can pressure to do one thing bring an avoidance
of pressure to do another?
How can the symptoms of grave assumptions hold us
in their steadfastness and never let us go.

There is however a way out of this predicament,
but you have to be able to say the first line:

God, please help me to accept first aid being
rendered to me, for so many years I have been the
one to supplicate my own needs. Forgive me for
being so protective in the ownership of myself.
Teach me to let go and hand all my problems
over to you.

*Anne Hadley*

## CRUISING ROCK 'A' BILLY VAMPIRE

On essence of life we feed when we bleed
A pleasure you deceive,
On mortals we feed
Forms not mortal man or beast
Evil to some undead, immortal,
Embrace the vampire clan,

We exist to rock and roll strutting and strolling
Wrecking and cruising these streets,
Party animals true to our flesh,
Slickbacked jiving in heaving halls
Cruising our hot rod stacked cider,
Catch a bite on the road,

Rockabilly jives and parties all night long;
We race caddies 'n' rods till dawn
Cider drank we crawl home,
To rest out weary heads in a coffin made for two,
The rockabillys two,
Till another sunset wakes our embrace.

*K M Clemo*

## THE WOMAN WITH NO NAME

When all was said and done
The meagre spoils of two lives gone
Were scrutinised.

Half guiltily they opened rusty tins, containing badges, medals;
Prised apart the musty, fragile leftovers of wartime living;
Ration books reminding of the 'National Dried'
And sweetened orange world they once inhabited.

Photos, dog-eared, of a handsome, youthful sergeant,
Set against the desert background of the East.
Others of an old, young woman and her son;
The girl severe, bespectacled,
Her youthful joy snatched from her
As it had been from the sergeant's colleagues up the line.

Deep within the bundle
Lay another, unknown woman,
Young and fresh, fair curls
Around a face unburdened by the cares of war.
There was no name recorded on the back
To link her with the soldier and his past - or present.
Had they met too late,
When passion's aftermath had planned his future path?
And did the woman with no smile,
Their mother,
Know that she was there among the bundle
In-between them forty years or more?

They shared the pictures of their parents,
Framed and set them, plastic-covered, in their photo books.
And no-one recollected where the picture of the unknown woman went.
But then, what difference had she made
When all was said and done?

***Dee Yates***

## NIGHT CREATURES

Shadows crouch:
leisured ease
cats curl up
asleep on the snow.
Comes afternoon
siesta time
soon cats awake
moving slow.
Stretch out
hurry, scurry,
slink in gliding;
across the roof
through the night
luxuriously, simply hiding.
Some secret
assignation
dark shadows in flight;
streaking, sneaking
sinuously into
darkness of the night.

*T Webster*

## My Lassie

As I wandered through the heather
In the quiet of the glen
There I saw my lassie
I loved her I knew then

As the wind was gently blowing
The ribbon in her hair
Then she turned to greet me
She looked so sweet and fair

Her hand in mine I took then
And time it drifted by
Together then we wandered
In the quiet of the glen

We stood before the altar
Our vows we said and then
I took my lassie home
To the quiet of the glen

We lived our lives together
As the years went slowly by
Wandering through the heather
In the quiet of the glen

I went on before her
Until we meet again
When we can go a wandering
In the quiet of heaven's glen

I waited there to greet her
And we were young again
And so we go a wandering
In the quiet of heaven's glen.

**L E Davies**

## IN KEW GARDENS

Weary December smiles again,
Gracing a lawn where leaves have lain,
Been pelted by relentless rain
   And herded into piles.
And here behold, upon a seat,
A hungry tramp that comes to eat,
And rest a while his sorry feet,
   From roaming many miles.

Sat in a nook, he faces west,
Soon to be joined by a neater guest,
A timid robin, with orange breast,
   And a plaintive whisp'ring flute.
Confidingly the creature teems,
With melodies, in pearly streams,
Happy with nonchalant tender themes,
   But watchful and astute.

With gusto now, the man is munching,
Biting, crunching, liking lunching,
Pauvre robin, shoulders hunching,
   Lacking but a crumb!
Whatever next? Another guest!
Another songster, dapper dressed,
In black and white, with olive vest,
   And magic on his tongue.

To test their trust, at least to try,
He primes his palm with a piece of pie,
Gone, by gosh! In the blink of an eye,
   Along with the blacker sprite.
That blessèd talon touched his hand!
Smote his heart, a tiny stand,
That left its mark, unearthly brand,
   Long after with delight.

*Terence Belford*

## HOLIDAY TREASURE

In Spain,
A boat trip -
Not very far,
Only to Lloret
From Tossa De mar,
A wonderful sight
I saw that day.
Mini rainbows
In the spray.
Even as I glimpsed them,
They were gone!
But happily, others
Came along,
Transient, iridescent,
Dancing in prancing foam
One second,
Yet in my memory
Finding a home!

***Vera Sykes***

## MY BROKEN HEART
*(Letter to Richard Madeley and Judy Finnegan)*

Here is my heart, broken in two.
Because I lost my chance to appear with you.
The greatest chance in my life, I've ever had,
To talk about my writing although it's sad
To meet Denise again, the signed photo she gave me in '95
Hangs on our kitchen wall with great pride,
I would never have gone on holiday to Skegness,
If I had known the outcome would have caused me such distress,
To be contacted three times by your then researcher,
Nicola McNelous
To be asked to appear on your show as a guest.
It broke my heart. When I found all her messages, but by then too late
I would have come back from my holidays.
Done anything to keep that date
I watch your show every day,
Please God let them give me another chance I pray,
I would give anything in this world to be,
Sitting with my husband with you two on that settee,
With my eighteen-year tranquilliser addiction and agoraphobia,
I've been to hell and back,
But now my life is back on track.
I give hope to others, to show the world what I have done,
Who knows it may even be fun.
So please Richard and Judy, answer my prayer,
Please, please, please, let us be there.

*Pat Dring*

## THE GREAT RACE!

Two schoolboys had some curious pets
Which raced at end of term;
One pet was a millipede,
The other was a worm.

The whole school got excited,
And many bets were placed;
Then all went to the playing field
In time to watch the race.

This race, though, was a non-event:
Worm tangled with some roots,
And millipede took far too long
To lace up all his boots!

*Roger Williams*

## EDUCATING SUSIE

'Spastic, mentally-handicapped, ineducable',
A harsh diagnosis for one so small,
The bottom suddenly dropped out of my world,
For her, life offered nothing at all!

Not speak, not able to communicate?
Unable to know, to learn, to read?
Never to experience the wonder of books,
In my mind God then planted a seed.

On that day long ago, He gave me a task,
To educate a daughter others might shun,
Beginnings were small, yet each a success,
Years before she could walk, never run!

Coloured picture books, a starting point,
Patience, repetition, dragging words off her tongue,
Stories explained, talked and laughed about,
Susie's education had begun!

Soon a teenager and middle-aged Mum
Were building up words with letter blocks,
Learning the alphabet has names and sounds,
Discovering dyslexia - another huge shock!

During what I thought were empty years,
When progress seemed almost nil,
Her mind was absorbing so much around
And her tongue was now never still!

That seed sown has grown like the mustard tree,
A seventy year old woman listens with love
To her forty year old daughter reading stories,
While prayerfully thanking the Headmaster above.

*Pat Heppel*

## ROOM FOR IMPROVEMENT

God looked on Creation,
Heaven and Earth,
Sun and Moon, sky and stars
Plants and animals
And man
And found it . . . fairly good.
'Not bad, not bad at all,
But there's room for improvement,'
She said.
And God made Woman.

This time she went easy on the brute strength
Gave instead a serpent's cunning,
The tigress' tenacity in defence of her cubs,
The power to hear what is not said
And see what is not visible.
Human Being Mark two.
'A definite improvement,' said God.

*Mary Hodges*

## ALONE

Sometimes when on your own and you feel that nobody cared
You will find someone with sincere feelings and the understanding
                                              is shared
When respect and courtesy, important in anyone's book
Comes first and foremost as you can tell from the way that they look
The special people who say 'Hello', not just because of who you are
But those considerate, though you are not near or afar

When alone people need friends, guys and gals
Special people who you can sincerely call your pals!
Trustworthy and true to confide in and respect
Such people are rare, falseness is so easy to detect,
When one is so lucky to find 'diamonds' so rare
You then share your life, love and truth stripped bare.

To all those alone I will always understand
For I am the same but my life 'He' commands!
The confidence I have is that someone shares
The joy that I feel knowing that somebody cares
When a birthday is remembered and treated with joy
And I look back with gratitude to when I was a boy
How do I thank all those who were then involved
Lovely times remembered with 'umpteen' problems, many
                                               still unsolved

To all those alone, have courage, never fear,
You will always find someone, so kind, so very near.
So give your love and friendship no matter what the cost
For without them you will be helpless, hopelessly lost,
Love all who respect you and return it as trust has grown
Because they are your life and with them you are never *'alone'*!

*Tony W Rylatt*

# A Letter Home

Mum, Dad come and get me please,
I spend most of my time on my knees.
My feet are swollen and my boots are tight,
I'm so cold, I can't sleep at night.
My clothes are so wet, they are never dry,
All I want to do is curl up and cry.
The owls are screeching in the trees,
It sounds so eerie, I wish I could scream,
Shadows, shadows are everywhere,
They're so huge, I can't compare.
My heart is beating really loudly,
Hope you don't think I'm being cowardly.
The rats are so big and they stare at me,
They eat their share of my tea.
Tomorrow, I've been told, I have to fight,
I don't want to kill anybody, but I know I might.
Mum, Dad, there's blood everywhere,
Men are dying, I can swear.
People are screaming from their pain,
Now the weather's changed, it's starting to rain.
Our trenches are wet and full of mud,
There's nowhere to hide, Mum, it's making my poor head thud.
Gunfire cracks through the night,
The bullet speeds out with a small bright light.
The cannons boom and then jump back,
One landed on my best friend Jack.
He is lucky, he's out of this war,
Mum, Dad, I can't take anymore.
Every time I close my eyes,
I try to imagine I'm by your sides.
I hope tomorrow will never come,
But I do know I must not run.

I must stand up and be a man,
And fight my country and protect the land.
Mum, Dad the day is here,
I must go into battle, I'm full of fear.
I'm so scared, I look at the sky,
It's full of gun smoke and cannon fire.
My comrades fallen to my left,
Now the one had fallen to my right.
The earth sticks to me like clay,
Mum, Dad, oh why did I have to lie about my age?
Wire, wire, it's everywhere,
With bodies hanging on it, all I can do is stand and stare.
There's a misty cloud all around,
Ouch! I've been hit, I'm on the ground.
Mum, Dad, I can't write anymore,
It's getting dark, I'm dying for sure.
I'm trying hard to be really brave,
But in my head I can see my grave.
Mum, Dad, I love you both,
Hope you get my letter in the post.
My eyesight is fading among the smoke,
Please give my dog Ben one last stroke.

John

Your ever-loving son,
Dopey John, 'who never should have gone'.

*Kayleigh Rhodes (15)*

## MY HOME WORLD

'Come, walk with me.' the Master said,
gently lifting up my head.
He walked and talked and laughed with me,
His gaze so pure twinkled merrily.

He took me on a tour of His land,
guiding my arm with His nail-scarred hand.
Each step He took with His nail-scarred feet,
left beautiful flowers with a perfume so sweet.

Although it took no effort at all,
we seemed to climb a mountain tall.
Where we beheld a panoramic view,
of African, Arabian, Caucasian, Indian people to name but a few.

A patchwork of faces from every land,
turned as one, as he lifted His hand.
Chattering, smiling happily,
they worshipped Him and welcomed me!

'Another of My beloved has come,
her work is o'er, her race is run.
Each of you who are so precious to Me,
spend time with her and show her love ever free.'

And so into the kingdom I was welcomed in,
with love and smiles and hugs, my heart was full to the brim.
Everything was perfection, no ugliness here,
it was nothing to do with how things looked -
just that sin could not draw near.

No illness, no pain, no tears, no death,
just health, vitality and peace drawn in with every breath.
Plants and animals, insects and birds, all of nature was here,
the best the world had held had been a pale reflection it would appear!

Then I was led to a hall of splendour, such as I had never known,
my Father who created me, embraced me saying, 'Welcome home!'

*Margi Hughes*

## NOT A LITTLE SPARROW FALLETH

As my friend and I to church did go,
we glanced upon the ground.
And there we saw a small swallow,
just crying to be found.
Gently I lifted the quivering bird,
and clasped it to me near.
Whispering; 'Please don't cry, our Lord has heard,
he knows your needs, so do not fear.
The little bird had straw entwined,
around its wing and claw.
We looked, and then the vicar did find,
he took us through the church door.
'Our Lord knows the needs of His little child,'
the vicar did exclaim.
'In His mercy so tender and mild,
you were found in His sweet name.'
The vicar cut away the straw,
from the tiny bird's claw and wing.
The little swallow was free once more,
to fly and God's praises to sing.
The little swallow flew away,
so thankful to be free.
I knew I'd never forget this day,
when God sent this little one to me.
Rejoicing we went back into church to pray,
feeling God's love all around.
The vicar gave thanks for the beautiful way,
that God's divine love did abound.
Jesus said; 'The Father knows the need,
of His creatures both great and small.'
His divine love is with us indeed,
and envelops us one and all.

Now as I stroll along the lane,
and hear the birds sing in the trees.
I whisper, 'Lord If you need us again,
please whisper to us in the breeze.'

*Nicky Young*

## MAYTIME MAGIC

May is a wonderful month in our town -
Winter retreats before bright flowers,
With their promise of long sunny hours . . .
While long and lissom limbs turn warm nut-brown.

Each semi's garden dons a bright new gown,
In which are hid secret and delightful bowers
Where shelter may be sought when sudden showers
Bring unexpected brief refreshments down.

This month, somehow, our hearts are set aglow
With sheer delight, as happy thrushes sing
Sweet hymns of joy in morning's rosy flush . . .
And we rejoice as from his high plateau
The sun slides west on all day's blossoming,
To hear our prayers of thanks at evening hush.

*Dan Pugh*

## DAWN RAID

In the far distance,
Through the mist of the early morning
The arrow-straight line fast approaches.
Strong, determined, intimidating, unswerving,
The brave leader prepares the troops for attack.
The sound of their voices penetrates the stillness.
Crossing the field their speed accelerates,
As they approach the low trees
They break ranks,
And with a cacophony of battle cries
They swoop unmercifully towards their prey,
Pushing and shoving, they devour . . .
Bread, on the dew-sparkling grass.
It's breakfast-time for the ducks!

*Joan Thompson*

## FAMILY PHOTOGRAPH

In her eighties,
this old frail woman
has survived a stroke,
her body shortened
and she is stooped.
Two row of pearls glow
over her navy blouse,
while quietly -
her six foot son,
once a baby in her arms,
now a father -
takes her by the hand
and walks to the door
of her home,
where I click the camera
capturing a moment
in a photograph,
before the final lunch
of a mother with her family.

*Mary Guckian*

## IT WAS SO BEAUTIFUL

The way lay treacherous beyond the stones
Of granite, wide and long
And the noonday sun burned down upon my head and
    the wind made many moans

In spite of all the pitfalls that appeared to be
    miraculously there
My heart told me to carry on
The way lay treacherous beyond the stones

Deep stone steps appeared from nowhere
So hot, that they hurt my feet
And the noonday sun burned down upon my head and
    the wind made many moans

Venturing down the deep stone steps
A door was wide open at the bottom
The way lay treacherous beyond the stones

Standing in the doorway, the cavern was so beautiful
Lit by church candles at intervals
And the noonday sun burned down upon my head and
    the wind made many moans

The cavern walls were covered with ancient tapestries
And a magnificent statue of Jesus Christ stood in the
    centre of the ancient carpeted floor
The way lay treacherous beyond the stones
And the noonday sun burned down upon my head and
    the wind made many moans.

*Alma Montgomery Frank*

## MORE THAN WORDS!

Restless, energyless and numbness to pain,
tiresome, insomnia they all sound the same.
The *highs* hang loosely as if ready to bolt,
when the *lows* creep unpredictably almost,
as if from within some deep dark unfocused
corner of the mind.
You cannot hear them or even see them,
those *lows of mood* . . .
You know the ones . . . !
They chew you up and spit you out and
all that's left is the headache, the tension
and that knotted nauseous feeling right
in the pit of your stomach.

An ache that stretches its entirety from
head to neck then neck to arm,
Through long bones and short bones until
it reaches your legs, feet and toes -
then circumnavigates your body again.
Medication in the morning, lunchtimes,
tea times and at night.
Anti-depressants, antipsychotics, Ativan
and such like.
Tablets for this and tablets for that,
just to be able to function alright!
I guess I must be profoundly *sad*
or even a tad depressed.
Such is the life on the medication
magical roundabout.
No way on and no way off, just round
and round and round it goes,
Where it will stop, nobody knows!

*Lyn M Jones*

## FRIEND

A friend I knew walked by today
It made me feel downcast,
But, when she turned and came to me
The time sped by so fast.
Her joy and sparkle cheered me up,
With such friends we cannot fail,
As she turned to go, I waved my hand
And she,
Just wagged her tail!

*E Osmand*

## RUSH HOUR TRAGEDY

A grey-haired, prim old lady
Sat, as old ladies do,
In a non-smoker's carriage,
Her name was Miss Magroo.

The train was travelling in the rush hour
To a station near Golders Green
And it was full to capacity
As it had often been.

She smiled as she pushed her way
Through the crowds of well-dressed men,
Carrying her umbrella beside her
Which tapped them, now and then.

She descended from the train,
Into a porter pushing a trolley.
Said 'Young man, look where you're going!'
Then hit him with her brolly.

*Joyce Walker*

## WAR MUSIC

Across the backs of the years
Kings break like reeds

Ascendant, vanquished,
In a chronicle of implacable feuding.

This war butchery never abates,
Lust for dominion is infinite.

Sanctified men have blood-drenched these parishes,

The centuries planted a raven battle flag
On these monster-haunted fens,

Till history tells of two rage-blind soldiers
Whacking each other with shovels.

Such times do not fade.
The sun still spills in the sky
With the gore of conquest

Until on every page of our annals
There is blood, ash.
Such brutal war music.

*Robert James Berry*

## YOUR BABY GIRL

Of all the years you spend on earth
Your greatest day was giving birth,
Could you believe that special morn
Your darling little girl was born . . . ?

Her pink array, your suckled breast,
Hey Mother, you know you've been blessed,
Your little angel snug and warm,
She knows you'll keep her safe from harm.

Can you believe those trusting eyes,
Your tears of joy - a thousand sighs,
You just behold as there she lies,
You'll never have a greater prize.

A loving bundle in her cot,
You give her all the love you've got,
You love her with a mother's heart,
Ensuring that you'll never part.

And father's heart has burst with pride
He's got two angels by his side,
Your world complete, a threefold love,
You've got to thank the Lord above.

The years will come, the years will go,
Life's sorrows ebb, life's joys will flow,
One thing you cannot place above,
That girl returning mother's love.

**Seph T October**

## THE DREAM

What do I see through your eyes?

The shimmering sea.
The sea shimmering, it glitters by daylight.
The sea shimmering, it whispers by moonlight.
Becalmed, the horizon pales to a blue haze and then to nothing.

The raging sea.
The sea raging, with froth and weed, it beats the shore senseless.
The sea raging, frothing, it crashes the shore relentless.
And yet this unrelenting pace stills my soul and my mind.

A wave has no end.

The deep blue sea,
The blue sea deep falling fathoms to silence,
The blue sea deep clear waters coloured by azure.
Looking seaward, the warmth of the sun on your face as my spirit
                                                                       drifts by.

What do I see through your eyes?
A glimpse of you and I.

***Sudha Patrick***

## TRACES

There is evidence of blood here.
Ask yourself why?
A finger has been pricked,
There is broken glass
Slivers linger yet.
Traces of a domestic scene,
Presupposing voices raised,
No, maybe only one.
We cannot say with certainty
Violence, yes,
Then likely some remorse,
Or else, where is the glass?
The picture of a loved one or a place,
A shattered frame, a desecrated face,
Gone. Too severely damaged to ever be restored.

Would analysis reveal the salt of spattered tears?
Are there traces of a trauma captured here?
You must decide.

Tell me:
Do you feel the ghosts of sad despair,
Or, 'Hold me tight,'
And reconciliation in the air?

*John Tirebuck*

## THE RUNAWAY HORSES

Along the countryside I go,
Should I go fast or should I go slow?
Suddenly I feel a great gust of wind go past
Well goodness me it seemed so fast.

But then when I look up to see,
It was a horse galloping past me.
Then before I had time to look away
I saw it was coming straight for me. Help! I pray.

The galloping of the horses are like thunder,
What are they running from I wonder?
I can almost feel the hot breath as they close in,
Their heads are almost touching my chin.

I close my eyes and hope for the best,
I feel a thud against my chest.
Dare I open my eyes and see what's there.
Then I hear peoples' cries of cheer.

I'm in the arms of a tall strapping man.
Who also has a wonderful tan.
'What happened?' I say, still in shock.
'You were lucky, you almost hit that rock.'

The horses galloped away because they were in fright.
The cows tried to stampede them as they got out in the night.
So as I sit here, my senses I try to regain,
I feel relief as I look at my hero again.

*Kathy Buckley*

## THE ABORIGINE AND THE JEWEL

Where corals lie, the diver swims
Bronzed and dark, the Aborigine.
North east of the Great Divide
In the Pacific Ocean, the Aborigine
Sinks and searches for the marine jewel.
The coral, the awesome presence
Growing and evolving 'neath the sea
The red reef, the coral reef
Sometimes white, sometimes pink.
Tropical fish waft and float
Around its beauty in the deep of the ocean
Colourful streaks of turquoise
Orange, blue and yellow.
Darting here, darting there.
At home in their habitat
Tropical fish, darting and free
Under the sea
Where corals lie, the octopus pumps
And swoops like a mumpish mushroom.
The white shark and the dolphin rise
And soar 'neath the sea, skim
Enchanting, enchanted, enchanting
'Neath the clear sunlit water
Of the Pacific, where corals lie.

*Margaret Bennett*

## DEVONSHIRE DOWNS

Out at last from towns abound.
Out at last to freedom found.
Leaving the Forge at Cockington Village,
We started forth -
Not on foot this time, alas, we had trodden -
Them aghast.
Up and down, in and out,
Around the Coves of Torbay past.

O rolling downs we see at last,
Upon you our eyes to feast,
While in peace our feet remain -
Until we reach Buckfast domain,
What beauty did our Creator paint?
'Tis easy to see that peace was meant,
For all and sundry to live in content.
With breeze to blow and bees to buzz.
Sheep to graze amid the maize -
Of footpaths trodden down by ponies.

The Abbey pinnacles arise in distance, not too far.
At last we alight with eagerness,
To view the beauty of this sight.
So neatly built and cleanly kept, by no more -
Than six Benedict Monks adept,
Did they build this site, brick by brick
Until the light out of sight came through the windows
They had created with delight?
God blessed their work, their home for life will remain -
Surrounded by Devonshire Downs.

*Joan Beedle*

## SPIDER IN HIS WEB

The dew was sparkling on the spider's web
Showing twinkling, sparkling, delicate threads
Crystal magic was everywhere

Living in your web so dramatically designed
Intricately woven, spun to perfection
The widow lady awaits
What a huntress, fearless and brave

***Kate Davies***

## THE CLYDESDALES

When I was a child of eleven years,
I was sent on an errand by my parents,
A distance of two miles or so,
It seemed much more than that.

The sun was hot and I was tired,
When I came to this field and thought
If I go through at the west side,
Follow a straight line to the east.

This would shorten my journey there,
I could see no animals in this field,
So, crawled through the barbed fence,
Then half-way across, I heard it

A noise like a herd of elephants stampeding,
To my horror, two Clydesdale horses were
Thud! Thud! Thudding their way towards me,
The ground beneath me shook and vibrated,

Spurring me on to reach my goal,
As fast as my jelly-like legs could go,
I did not look back, fear kept me going
Right over the fence to safety.

Once there, I paused for a short breath,
On taking one last look at the horses,
Was amazed to see them right there,
In what seemed no distance at all.

The look on their faces as if to say,
Why were you running away from two friends,
At that moment, I realised they meant no harm,
All that was required was a soothing voice,
A caress or two, someone to take time to talk,
Just like humans, they want companionship.

*Mary Lawson*

## WHITE SILK

There were paintings of horses with high flaring nostrils,
Rearing on battlefields long, long ago:
Children with ringlets and white lacy collars,
Shoe trimmed with buckle or slipper with bow.

In his gilt frame a duke stood, enrobed in red velvet,
Holding a scroll in one ruby-ringed hand;
Nearby a hunt in full cry over hedgerows
Long gone, uprooted in road greed for land . . .

Here a family portrait, with plump placid parents,
Bonneted baby upon Mother's knee;
Proud Father's hand on his little son's shoulder,
None of the scene lacking some finery.

Smooth polished wood shone, where chandelier crystal
Cast glittering light on a bureau or chair;
Books with frail bindings graced shelves in a study,
Touching forbidden - but then, who would dare . . . ?

Now at last, the great portrait that stilled all the murmurs,
Present-day Venus, from stray curl to toe,
Glowing in gown of white silk, newly fashioned
Worn just for him, not that others would know . . .

Not that others would know of her love for the artist,
Why from her eyes such sweet radiance was shed;
Not for the duke she was destined to marry
But for another in secret to wed . . .

In her gown of white silk she had married her true love.
Gone is the portrait from Stately Home wall.
Somewhere an artist paints Mother and Baby
Lovingly, simply: his best work of all.

*Mary Cane*

## REFUGEES

I learned from the elders
I learned about their agony
'A man without a country
Is a man without dignity'
Was what I was taught as a child
The people around me
Were my people
Broken people
Scattered
Disposed
Powerless
In my head they sowed a dream
The desire of returning
The desire that never fades
The desire that is presently out of reach
Instead a new generation
Stands in the shadows of the elders
Watching, waiting, wanting

***K Parveen-Mirza***

## THE RENOVATION

People came from far and wide to have a look - to see inside
The house they made as good as new, its popularity slowly grew.
The door was slammed over again, as they arrived in droves of ten
To watch the bricky build his wall, and the old one demolished and fall.
Three weeks of Hell will soon be four, first of all they moved the door,
Now a window stands in place and of that door there is no trace.
They ripped out windows and put in new, replaced the bath,
sink and loo
Ripped up floorboards rotten with worm, just the thought to make
me squirm.
The sparkie came and did his bit, a pretty nice job I must admit.
A chippy hung the exterior door, the rain seeps in and soaks the floor.
The living room is out of bounds, no longer can I watch the
postman's rounds.
The door won't shut it needs a shave, now the walls we have to save,
The kitchen stands stripped and stark, the appliances stand alone
in the dark.
We sit and watch the black and white in our bedroom every night.
As we sit in despair and wait, for the end, to celebrate.
For all the work in hand be done, this experience is not much fun.
Workmen stand round drinking cups of tea, discussing the state
of our economy,
Messing around with bits of wood and not doing the job they should.
We live in a bedroom, all cramped in, until the structural engineer
has been
To have a look at the supporting beam, this is a nightmare
within a dream,
This experience I have to say, is a nightmare every day,
If you wish for a renovation, just read this poem of my frustration.

*Marcus Tyler*

## THE PAIN OF FAME

Child's desire to perform and please
Sisterly rivalry, mother's drive.
Spurred on by talent,
relentlessly striving.
Village hall to concert platform,
little town to world renown.

Cello and Du Pre became as one,
vibrating and melodic.
Creation by God, composer and Jackie,
in Elgar's Cello Concerto.
Autumnal introspection and melancholy,
were mirrored in her life.

Third movement's plaintiff melodies
Cello's solo splendour,
wallowing in mournful notes.
Triumphant in last movement,
loudness reflecting quiet phrases,
spiritually exhausting.

Frustration, deep despair,
shaking, loss of control.
Disobedient fingers,
crippled by MS.
Husband's loving care,
but . . . death the final conductor.

*Ray Rippingale*

## MARRIED BLISS

It's left me feeling broken hearted,
He didn't seem to care,
We just felt like strangers,
He didn't notice I was there.
I can see now his beloved face,
Something you can't forget,
I'll always remember our joy and pride,
When we saw that house to let.
We papered and we plastered,
We scrubbed away and painted,
But what we never realised,
Was that love can soon be tainted.
Fortunately we hadn't children,
With whom our life to share,
If that wondrous thing had happened,
It would have been more than I could bear.
Then one night I made a meal,
A very special birthday treat,
I'd made a cake with candles,
All we had to do, was eat.
He came in very late that night,
Said he was working late,
Even then I never realised,
This was a cruel act of fate!
He'd met a curvy bottle blonde,
She'd completely turned his head,
After many months of pain and lies,
I realised our love was dead.
Never take things for granted,
Just be happy, whilst you can.
My idol had got feet of clay
Not now my lover - just a man!

**Edith Antrobus**

## SUMMER TIME

It was evening, after a long hard day
An evening in summer, down a leafy lane
A sultry time, with the smell of hay
Of newly cut corn. And harvest, once again.

Then I met her and caught her eye
Just for an instant, but it was enough
I looked for her the following night, asking why
Would she be interested in a lad like I?

Not a romp in the hay with all the fun
But the beginning of something, not knowing what.
We met a lot after that, in the summer sun
Not realising what we had got.

Getting to know each other was lots of fun
Not easy at first, the words wouldn't come.
And I thought too much of her to cut and run
When she suggested that I should meet her mum.

Mum was pleased, for she had no son
Her dad was so quiet, I knew I was (in),
Then mum took over, her work just begun
Wedding bells in the distance, she knew she had won.

We wed in the spring, had a place of our own
Not easy, with all the trials, the laughter and tears.
The young ones not young anymore, my how they've grown
And my thoughts go back to those early years.

Now mum has gone, and dad has a frame
I do not think of the future, amidst the fears
It is so sad that nothing can remain the same
But I still have my thoughts of those early years.

*K R French*

## THE SOUP - TIN WAY

Do you see young Joe
Tapping his toe to commercial radio?
Paling in the passenger seat, sweating on a fifth lung,
Waiting for his turn and his money's worth
From a trip that will start down off the back of his tongue.

He's an English member
Of my generation's apathetic gender.
Born as the Rotten sneer was becoming parody
And the desire to change anything other than your pin-stripe suit
Disappeared from your veins replaced with yuppie flu and salary.

Now our average Joe is today's job-seeking youth
Warmed in flea-pit excelsis by a similarly aged two-bar heater.
Nasal passages lighter fuel soothed,
In a fantasy realm he dreams of a tambourine,
Strutting his stuff on stage and the funky music he'd play.
He could be the one to sing the rebel song for a worthy rebel cause,
To re-ignite what should have been finished and scream;
'Let the rebellion start with me.'
Or maybe he will, on another day.
If there is any bile, desire and spleen left in him after the
Government sponsored training scheme.

Left to hide lethargy behind a CV
Of minimum wage and 'measured efficiency'.
It's another adult life spent excelling at the banal.
A diary worthy of being Warholian art;
A Marilyn screen-print holding together a mechanistic part.

We've got enough thin men called Jones, now can we have some heroes
Who won't back down and only wake up to smell the red rose?
We've been sold out for chart rundowns and teeny-bop wild excess.
We've been sold out by bronze celebrity skin and corporate press.
Does Bobby Charlton really make you *this* proud?

*Peter Clarke*

## FOOTBALL PLANS

Robert Smithers had a dream
To play football for a class team.
He practised each and every day,
He wouldn't study, he'd just play.

His mum would worry every day,
She'd often hear his teacher say,
'You need to work, to learn to read,
One day your maths' knowledge you'll need.'

But Robert smiled and would reply
Which only made his teacher sigh.
Some day I'll be a football star
With lots of money and a car.

He struggled with his reading books,
Impressed the girls with his good looks.
His football skills improved each year,
His tackles never showed his fear.

He feared failure most of all,
His greatest love was his football.
He'd train each day, he'd eat good food,
He'd always feel in a good mood.

He had a trial for a team,
There he discovered self esteem
Determination and his skill
Added together with self will
Enabled Robert to achieve
His football dream, not make believe.

*Catherine Craft*

## TRILOGY OF MOTHERHOOD

Eve

They stride boldly and stamp their watered feet,
proudly shaking engorged stomachs,
and lifting sagging breasts
that haunt their nights of a stone engraving
only whispered in their Motherhood Literature.
Secretly squeezing into a tighter skin,
they blow forwards to their dated relief,
and dance within their birthing peach.
'The helpless child
that will cling to them forever?'
Nagging slivers shake off their permanence,
softened through practical remedies,
backache, numbness, tingles and a black dreaded dream,
that weaves into the swollen days and nights of waiting.

During

Posed under the pinnacle of an arduous ascent,
women scream at new pain,
and their eyes grow glazed with bloodied shock,
as the child rips through their body
and spills out of their hearts.
Father cries, and attendants
pen the details of a new life and a routine birth.
The new mother lies in her juice,
as the warmth of a baby's lips
pulses and tugs at the tender nipple.
She tries to sleep, pupils tense
and hard staring into the future.
With a blinding vision.

Life

Giving, giving, giving,
living and rising in the nights of screaming darkness.
Smiling at friends,
and cuddling a sweet scented child.
Bathing, feeding, changing, playing, loving
against a clock with too few seconds.
Time escapes,
and you will find a new mother with her precious book
and warm waters to heal.
Too few seconds and the cry begins its relentless trail
into pain, sleep, tears and joy.
We fall in love
to sweetly tend to the ravenous child.
Father gives but can stand aside,
Mothers give and lose their friends,
their sharp edged clothes,
their sharp edged figures.
A new millennium and an independent life?

Someone has failed to explain,
how a child's passion
can be diffused that we may
sleep again within our own names.
Without a horrible guilt.

*Tina Coope*

## THE LIFE OF AN UNBORN CHILD

We watched the birth of the snowdrops at the start of the year,
Fussing over the lambs warned by the ewe not to go too near.
Spring had arrived with its magical colour,
And the pretty daffodils nodded to each other.

We rolled our Easter eggs down the hill,
Coloured by the gorse flower surrounding the mill,
Running excitedly through fields of bluebells,
The flowers shyly keep to themselves.

The heat of the sun forces buds into bloom,
As suddenly we are thrust into glorious June.
Wildlife surrounds us - mostly unseen,
How beautiful everything is when it's so green.

Strolling the shore and dodging the waves,
Collecting seashells and hunting for caves.
Watching for sea lions and waving to boats,
Notice how easy a seabird floats.

Harvest is upon us and we must make haste,
To collect nature's bounty and savour its taste.
Pots of home-made jam, we love to make,
And pies oozing with juice, we need to bake.

A child at Christmas is a joy to behold,
Before they suddenly grow too old.
And realise that Santa is part of a game,
We have lost the true story - now that is a shame.

These are but some of the things I would do,
If I had given birth to you.
In my heart this child was born,
But it will never live and I will always mourn.

*Valerie Caine*

## LIFE'S PROGRESS

At one a child's life has just begun,
At two they walk and talk and do.
At three they're lively, full of glee!
At four they learn to paint and draw.
At five it's school and time to thrive.
At six they're up to many tricks.
At seven they question the meaning of Heaven.
At eight they start to interrogate.
At nine their talents begin to shine,
At ten they learn to know just when
Things are right or wrong to do.

After that they grow up fast.
Babyhood over, childhood past.
As teenagers they know it all!
We watch them carefully lest they fall,
By twenty we hope a career's underway.
To college or work they soon go away.
Next come the partners, the highs and the lows,
Lessons in life, that's how it goes!
Next there are babies and life has begun
The same as it started when they were just one!

*Jan Edmunds*

## THE FACE

I first saw your small face
It was on a Friday
Crumpled with grumpy dreams.
I knew then that I would love you, reverently.
If there had been two white wings on your back,
I would not have batted an eye.
As you grow so does our bond of love, unconditional.
Your pain is my pain, your tears are mine,
As if cried from the same eyes.
I have never said the words 'I love you'
With such fortification.
Soppy, you have made me!
I remember it was on a Friday
I first saw your small face . . .

***D P R***

## SLENDER HARVEST

This year our cordon bore just one fruit.
Perfect and solitary,
It has pride of place on our dresser,
A whole harvest under one skin.
We must learn to divide our treasure
Or watch it rot before us.

My womanhood has borne little more:
Two fruits for all my years' blossoming.
The eldest grew firm and separate,
A little sharp perhaps, having a legal mind,
But with sweetness to delight.
Now her beauty is enjoyed by others.

Just one child remains to me,
Growing fair and straight.
My son, I would keep you longer,
Treasure you for my winter years,
But youth, like fruit, needs air.
For you too, I must wish ripeness,
And a maturer love.

*Pauline Kirk*

## To My Two Boys

You were born thirty years ago today,
and as you grew we watched you play.
We saw you grow big and very strong,
and watched you play all day long.
Then as time went by you changed
from being boys into fine young men.
Now you are grown up this very day
with homes and families of your own.
We had you on loan to us for a while
but then the time came when we had
to let you go to make your own way.
But even though this has come to us,
we still love you all the same today.

*John Harrold*

## WHO WOULD HAVE THEM?

Children - who would have them?
I've often heard this said.
They take all your money,
Leave you in the red.
From the moment of conception,
They give you sleepless nights,
It seems you spend each waking hour
Teaching wrong from right.
They never seem to listen,
Think they know what's best,
Forever try your patience,
Put it to the test.

Children - who would have them?
They give you so much love,
Bring sunshine to your darkest days,
A gift from God above.
A cuddle when you're feeling low,
A song to make you smile,
A voice that's asking 'When?' and 'Why?'
Dependent all the while.
A little being that somehow,
Can make you feel so proud,
You're always saying 'That's my boy'
He stands out from the crowd.

So children - who would have them?
I'd do it all again,
Did I really say that?
Or am I quite insane?

*Jim Sargant*

## A Joyous Gift

There are no words to express the emotion
Felt in a parent's heart
Of such love and devotion
On a tiny miracle to impart.
From the moment you are laid in an arm
The joy is there to behold,
And the need to keep you from harm
In a loving family to enfold.
When from nursery we ran to meet
And tiny arms round neck did go,
Such tenderness felt as we did greet,
Hugging each other, rocking too and fro.
We tried to teach you right from wrong,
At school to play the game.
For childhood is not for very long
Which really is a shame.
In life there were sad times too
Where loomed a large black cloud,
But strength of mind pulled you through
Of which naturally we are proud.
Age does not matter in a parent's eye
You will always be our child,
And with contented smile we try
To remember fond memories in a mind filed.
Good health be your companion on life's way.
Our hope that love and support help too
For to enjoy life whilst you may.
We thank you for simply being just you.

**Tess Walton**

## THE JOY OF CHILDREN

I do not yet know the joy of children,
When I am older I may have one, two or even ten.

Some people are thirteen when they have a baby,
Or some are even younger maybe,
Others are thirty, forty even,
Then there's the names; Jody, Laura or Steven.

Although children are great they aren't always happy and having fun,
They have their tantrums and quiet moments just like everyone,
But all in all the good times rule out the bad,
And the happy times rule out the sad.

For now I am happy as a child myself, I am,
No responsibilities, I am able to do what I want, I can.

*Kelly Harding  (14)*

# GOLD

*(Dedicated to my wonderful nephew Jordan on your*
*Christening day, twenty-ninth of April 2001 with all*
*My love always Auntie Tracy xxxxxxx)*

Of all the treasures possessed by man,
From sea to sea and land to land,
There is none that truly can compare . . .
As to the golden curls of infants' hair,
Though man may hike for countless miles,
Over hill and dale and wooden stile,
He'll find no light that shines as bright . . .
As his child's golden smile . . . lighting the darkest night,
Many men may search their whole life long,
For jewelled trinkets . . . wine and song,
Priceless treasures they may behold,
At rainbow's end . . . their pot of gold,
I hold my treasure close to my breast,
I need not indulge in foolish quests,
For in my arms I tenderly hold . . .
You my child . . . 18 carat gold.

*Tracy Bell*

## ALMOST!

A bundle to cuddle, a bundle to love
Now gone from me, to abide above,
A life curtailed, though little had ailed
A planned for future - but alas we failed.
A pregnancy started, but now departed
Meant to be with us - we are broken hearted
A little one expected, endeared throughout
Who could not survive when it came about
A loss to a mother - or no son for Dad,
Nor a daughter, what happened shouldn't oughter
Leaving we parents so lost and sad,
Newly named being - now not seeing
We try so hard to be staunch and brave
Gone to another - sister or brother.
Please dear Lord a place for it do save
Little bundle of joy, all our very own
Still human beings we all have feelings
A few short months to us was known.
We can't stop crying - over the 'goodbying'
Always recalling oncoming joy
Of the one approaching, on world encroaching
Lots of time ahead to thrill or annoy
You were wanted, now we are haunted
Was a bundle to cuddle, together we huddle
Such a pity that you have to go astray
We foretold you, wish we could hold you
Still it was an important day
A bundle to cuddle - but no chance to live,
We sought your love now Lord above
Our error or failure - please we forgive,
In times ahead we'll be so forlorn
A baby coming - oh so stunning - but alas *stillborn*!

*John L Wright*

# I Miss The Children

I miss the children, I miss their noise
Crying, laughing - playing with their toys
Bath times - and story times
I'd tuck them up - kiss them goodnight

And I'll never forget their school days
Living through their childhood phase
In their teens they had their dreams
Their hormones kicked to smithereens
Those mornings getting ready for school
Breakfast sounds - acting the fool
I'd watch them walking down the street
And they'd all turn and wave to me

And yes we loved our holidays
We had our favourite summer place
On the golden beach - splashing in the sea
Excited children would shout and scream

Yes, I really miss the children
And sometimes I feel so sad
I guess I'll always miss the children
The children I never had . . .

*Frank Howarth-Hynes*

## THE JOY OF CHILDREN

The day they are born they are pink and cute,
But also nice and cuddly until they puke.

They give us a big smile that makes us happy,
But OOPS it's time to change their nappy.

The faces we pull to make them laugh,
Then we decide they need a bath.

We count all ten fingers and ten tiny toes,
They are so perfect as they grow.

We help them learn from wrong and right,
We never let them out of our sight.

As they get older it gets harder every time,
To let them go and have some play time.

We must now take the time and watch our children grow,
For they are special to us as we do know.

*Jamie Brooks*

## CAN I WAIT?

Right . . .

> There's scribbles on the walls again
> Juice has stained the floor
> Smeared fingers on the windowpane
> Believe me . . . there's more.
>
> The toilet seat is left puddled
> The front door key is lost
> Unwatched Rugrats are blaring
> Wonder how much new trainers cost.
>
> Overfed dog has a sticky coat
> Messing about had made me late
> As usual they are being rude
> Me? Have kids? I can't wait.

*Or can I?*

**Stacey Tully**

## THE PARENTAL DILEMMA

A mother stands and looks on with pride
As her daughter wins her first race
And a tear falls as she hugs her so tight
Seeing the joy on her dear baby's face

Her little heart pounds with excitement
As she cries 'Mummy, I won, I won'
And her mother gently kisses her cheek
And thinks, 'That's one of her trials overcome'.

But the years ahead fill her with fear
To guide her child down the safest road
In this modern free and enlightened times
As the ascent to adulthood she grows

To turn her from drugs, cigarettes and drink
Or the abuse of solvents or glue
After the warnings, pleadings and threats
There is little more that a parent can do

By example you lead and hope your child learns
Peace of mind will come from only one way
That happiness comes from inside your heart
Earned by your own acts of kindness each day.

*Don Woods*

## TO MY CHILDREN

I cannot share your troubles
The crosses that you bear
But in trouble I am with you
And always will be there

My ears are yours to listen
My shoulder for your tears
My loving arms for comfort
When end of tether nears

I cannot share your troubles
That multiply and breed
But for sure I am a willing port
When you ever feel the need

When the storm clouds gather darkly
When day becomes the night
There is a far horizon
Where day is bathed in light

I cannot share your troubles
But good does follow bad
And when you need to bridge that gap
There's the hand of your old dad

You've given me much pleasure
You've made my life complete
What I can I'll do for you
To get your troubles beat

**Ray Ryan**

## MY TINY BUNDLE - OH WHAT JOY!

When that seed was planted, my heart cried out with joy.
And even more so, when I knew that he would be a boy.
I carried him inside me, so careful what I did.
I mustn't lose this treasure now, there's so much I must give.

Then he started nursery, I missed him all the way.
I really must be brave I thought, he must enjoy his day.
Next he went to school, at only four years old.
My little baby now was gone, my heart was filled with woe.
Never mind he'll come back, shortly after four.
I'll see his little smiling face there standing at the door.

Before I knew it, senior school was beckoning to him.
Then the big long trousers, it's really such a sin.
That little boy is six feet tall and looking down at me.
Next year he'll be far away at university.
He knows I'm feeling all alone, he's keeping it low key.
It doesn't seem a minute though since he sat on my knee.

Oh yes he's been a nuisance, coming in after six.
Playing heavy music and getting up to tricks.
Messing up the place, his bedroom such a tip.
That little seed so many times just gave me too much lip.

What more can I say now, except I must not cry.
Instead I must get on with life and let my sparrow fly.
I cherish all the memories, grateful that he's well.
Thank you Lord, I now have space, in fact I'm feeling swell!

*Geraldine Varey*

## My Grandad Keeps Penguins

'My grandad keeps penguins!'
The teacher smiled, 'You mean pigeons, dear.'
'No!' snapped the child.
'I mean penguins. He keeps them in his backyard -
Where I feed them with fish each day after school -
And watch them play in the paddling pool.'

'You'll be telling me next,' the teacher laughed -
'That your grandad keeps crocodiles under his bed!'
'Course not, Miss,' the child replied.
'They float in the bath -
And tigers and lions live in his shed.
Camels in the kitchen. Lizards in the lounge.
Parrots in the parlour. Hyenas always on the scrounge.
Bears in the bedroom and snakes coiled on the stairs.'

'Your grandad must live in a zoo!' said the teacher to the child.
'Otherwise, if not, your story can't be true.
Unless, of course, the animals are made of fur and cottonwool,
With glass beads for their eyes.'
'They're real!' The child began to cry -
'And I'm not telling lies!
Each one is my friend! Not like you! -
You're just pretend!'

To disbelieve a child however odd the tale -
Is to chip away a confidence still delicate and frail.
An invitation to a child's imagination -
Should be accepted without hesitation.
Open your eyes blinkered and blind -
Sweep the cobwebs and dust from your mind.
Re-enter a world you once knew so well -
Let the joy of a child weave its magical spell.

*Philip J Mee*

## TALKING

Why do people argue when,
it is easier to talk
and sort out all the differences.
To make a pleasant start.
Sometimes people like to hear
their voice and others are too shy.
But it doesn't matter what you like
It's the heart that really shows,
The peace and quiet and restfulness.
But children are so much great fun.
I could listen to all day,
But when they grow up things change.
So enjoy the joyful moments.
And grasp it right away.

***Heather Breadnam***

## PRECIOUS LULLABY

Little darlings loved and blessed
Joyful music swept caressed
Fingers clasped eyelids closed
Silken fabrics kiss your toes.
Special timbals salute your sighs
Smoothing the melody
Brightening the eyes
Kisses gentle
Lovingly ethereal
Fold your dimples
Pink and felicitous.

Luscious lips babbling
And garrulous.
Luminary light blissfully
Tranquil and sibylline
Morally undefiled
Accidentally serendipity
Talented goosander
Galloon binding dresses
Garniture guitars
Zesting gusto
Perfectly tuned.

Simple sincere unmixed
One little drop!
Droplets from the nubia
Ingeniously galactic
On the gamba of the
Delta and the garth.

**Sarah Margaret Munro**

## SALI

Rosy cheeks and curly hair,
Big blue eyes and skin so fair.
Four white stubbs of teeth in a grin,
A little diamond of dribble on her chin.
A chubby body that loves a tickle,
Your guaranteed to hear her giggle.
The unsteady aided stance,
Wobbly little legs that would love to dance,
Helpless without the care,
Unknowing, but with love to share,
Our little angel so precious and pure,
Without you, life would be dull,
That's for sure!

**Lloyd Hopkins**

## Summer

The trees are green the sky is blue.
Not a single cloud is in my view.
The flower beds are blooming too.

The wood pigeon's call is loud and clear.
The sparrows chirp for all to hear.
A group of starlings on the ground appear.

April's storms and rains seem far away.
It's a lovely, bright and sunny day.
I hope that summer's here to stay.

*B Eyre*

## THE COTTAGES

Four worn out old cottages huddle together,
Tormented and beaten by all kinds of weather,
Withstanding the torture that goes on forever.

Now no secrets remain where the cold wind has blown.
And windows stare blankly at the grass overgrown.
So forgotten, neglected they stand here alone.

But the seasons have changed and rain's tears kiss the ground.
Gentle wind now caresses the walls without sound,
And the sun beams his pleasure with warmth all around.

In the blossoming trees the birds sing their sweet song,
And wild, colourful flowers dance all summer long.
With this beautiful landscape all troubles seem gone.

As the laughter of children rebounds from the walls,
While they frighten each other with strange sounding calls.
This mysterious place now attracts and enthrals.

For these broken old ruins are not what they seem,
They help act as a focus for lovers to dream,
As the spirits of past lives float down a moonbeam . . .

*Sheila Maureen St Clair*

## The Tree

A seed by the wind blown
Becomes a tree fully grown
Casting a shade of its own.

Boys out on a spree
All climb up the tree
Swinging and shouting with glee.

Tree starts to bend
The boys hastily descend
The tree's sad end.

*Vicki Turner*

## IF ONLY

I love your face, I adore your smile
To see it I would run a two minute mile
Just to catch a glimpse, if only for a while

Your eyes shine like a deep sea pearl
Looking into them sends my heart in a whirl
Being next to you makes my toes curl

The touch of your hand sends me a shiver
My knees turn to jelly, I'm all of a quiver
A part of me loves you, if only a sliver

If only you could be mine to have and to hold
It would be the greatest story every told
To our children, together, as we grow old.

*Jane Bolderston*

## SLAVES SAVED (ABRIDGED)

'I pray you, Lord, my baby save
From drowning in a watery grave
On orders of that evil knave!'

God heard that mother's heartfelt prayer,
She hid her precious child with care
Trusting her God to guard him there.

God had his plan for that young life -
Not one for ease, but work and strife,
Where challenge and rebuff were rife.

The baby in the basket cried . . .
His hidden, watchful sister sighed.
A princess soon his basket spied!

Our Hebrew child was safe and sound,
In God's plan by a princess found;
As royal nurse, his Mother bound.

When grown a man, this Israelite
Moses, was angered by the sight
Of fellow countrymen's sad plight.

Their lives were made a hell on earth,
They felt no peace, no joy, no mirth,
Their very lives of little worth.

As slaves they laboured day by day
Fashioning bricks from Egypt's clay,
Fearing their captors' whip and flay.

Moses' assignment was quite tough:
'Tell Pharaoh God has had enough' . . .
It took ten plagues to call his bluff.

'You let my people go!' he said,
'Or God will strike your first-born dead.'
That done, the Israelites all fled.

*M A Sanders*

## THE FOUR SEASONS

We felt the warmth of log fires glow,
Saw robin's imprints in the snow
And watched the winter come and go.

But that was yesterday, now hark!
To the springtime trill of the little lark
And children playing in the park.

Summer - happy days we treasure,
Sunny hours of fun and leisure,
Season of immeasurable pleasure.

Hips and haws, bright golden grain,
Gathering blackberries down the lane,
Autumnal tints are here again.

So let us pause and reminisce
On all those seasonal moments of bliss
From Jan to December's mistletoe kiss!

*F Evelyn D Jones*

## JACK'S BEACH
*(Based on a painting by Jack Vettriano)*

Sand spreads like melted butter in the heat,
Two women paddle, cool their shoeless feet
and look to where the sky and ocean meet.

Cream parasols deflect the glaring sun,
air shimmers, making colours seem to run -
primrose, gold and ochre blend to one

long summer seascape, sweeping into view,
the distant water calm, its muted blue
a counterpoint to yellow's vibrant hue.

The women hitch their skirts above their knees,
like figures from some ancient Roman frieze,
athletic-limbed, Hellenic, bared to tease

their male companion, modesty attired -
straw hat and braces - Latin style inspired
by classic movies, dated but admired.

The scene lifts off the canvas, tells the eye
beyond the frame there's more than beach and sky -
the paint goes on, its colours not quite dry.

**Jean M Harvey**

# SUBMISSIONS INVITED
*SOMETHING FOR EVERYONE*

**POETRY NOW 2001** - Any subject, any style, any time.

**WOMENSWORDS 2001** - Strictly women, have your say the female way!

**STRONGWORDS 2001** - Warning! Age restriction, must be between 16-24, opinionated and have strong views. (Not for the faint-hearted)

All poems no longer than 30 lines.
Always welcome! No fee!
Cash Prizes to be won!

Mark your envelope (eg *Poetry Now*) **2001**
Send to:
Forward Press Ltd
Remus House, Coltsfoot Drive,
Peterborough, PE2 9JX

**OVER £10,000 POETRY PRIZES TO BE WON!**

Judging will take place in October 2001